GET OUTDOORS

Fishing

Nick Ross

WAYLAND

First published in 2008 by Wayland

Copyright © Wayland 2008

Wayland
338 Euston Road
London NW1 3BH

Wayland Australia
Level 17/207 Kent Street
Sydney NSW 2000

Senior editor: Jennifer Schofield
Designer: Rachel Hamdi and Holly Fulbrook
Photographer: Tudor Photography
Photoshoot co-ordinator: Rita Storey
Proofreader: Susie Brooks

Acknowledgements:
The author and publisher would like to thank the following people for participating in our photoshoot: Brian Syde (Banbury & District Angling Club), Mike Stanley, Rozie Stanley and Ben Rhodes.

A special thank you to Castaway Fishing Tackle, Banbury www.castawayfishing.co.uk for supplying equipment and to Justin Benjamin, Barry Ayers and Pete Ayers for supplying photographs.

All photography by Tudor Photography except
5 Bridgeman Art Library/Getty Images; 10, 11, 25 top, 25 left i-StockPhoto; 24, 29 top Luka Lukman; 28 Peter and Barry Ayers; 29 bottom Georgette Douwma/Getty Images

British Library Cataloguing in Publication Data
Ross, Nick
Fishing. - (Get outdoors)
1. Fishing - Juvenile literature
I. Title
799.1

ISBN: 978 0 7502 5058 0

Printed in China

Wayland is a division of Hachette Children's Books,
an Hachette Livre UK company.
www.hachettelivre.co.uk

Note to parents and teachers:

The website addresses (URLs) included in this book were valid at the time of going to press. However, because of the nature of the Internet, it is possible that some addresses may have changed, or sites may have changed or closed down since publication. While the Author and Publishers regret any inconvenience this may cause the readers, no responsibility for any such changes can be accepted by either the Author or the Publishers.

Disclaimer:
In preparation of this book, all due care has been exercised with regard to the advice, activities and techniques depicted. The Publishers regret that they can accept no liability for any loss or injury sustained. When learning a new sport, it is important to get expert tuition and to follow a manufacturer's advice.

Contents

The world of fishing 4

How to get started 6

Fishing equipment 8

Types of fish 10

Bait .12

Using the equipment 14

Basic techniques 16

Unhooking and returning a fish 18

Location, location, location 20

Types of fishing 22

Fly fishing and sea fishing 24

Clubs and competitions 26

Fish from around the world 28

Glossary 30

Further information 31

Index .32

The world of fishing

Fishing is a popular sport all around the world, with millions of people taking part. In the United Kingdom alone, nearly four million people, young and old, participate. Whether you are on your own, or with friends or family, fishing is a great way to relax and spend time outdoors having fun. There are many branches of the sport to choose from; with challenges for all – from the most physical and active people to those who like to sit quietly and enjoy the mental test of catching a fish.

Choosing a branch

Each branch of fishing involves different techniques and slightly different equipment. Fishing for trout or salmon is called fly fishing, or game fishing, while sea fishing takes place from the sea shore or off a boat or pier. The most popular branch of fishing is coarse fishing, which is fishing for freshwater fish, but not salmon and trout. Although this book looks at all three types, it focuses on coarse fishing.

Early beginnings

Apart from being one of the most popular sports in the world, fishing is also one of the oldest sports on record. Thousands of years ago, prehistoric people caught fish for food. They used hooks made from animal bone. Later, in the 1400s, rods were made from ash, hazel and willow wood, while lines were braided from horse hair.

Around the world, fishing is enjoyed by men, women, boys and girls.

Fishing equipment improved greatly after the Industrial Revolution in the eighteenth century and since then, rods and tackle have continued to develop to accommodate every sort of fishing imaginable.

Match Fishing

To catch fish you will need to concentrate, develop patience and think hard about what you are doing. Successful match fishermen plan well and are organized and skilled – they are able to change tactics to suit the water, type of fish and weather conditions. They learn to think like fish!

Fishing for food dates back thousands of years. This wall painting is from the Tomb Chapel of Menna in the Valley of Nobels in Thebes, in Ancient Egypt.

How to get started

There are many places to go fishing, from ponds and lakes specially made for fishing to canals and rivers, which have their own challenges. If you are over 12 years old, you may need to buy a fishing licence. Most fishing waters are owned privately or by an angling club, with many offering junior day tickets or season tickets. Sometimes clubs prefer young people to be accompanied by an adult so it is important to find out all the information you can before you set off.

Choosing the right water

Many lakes have prepared fishing areas called 'swims'. Look for a swim that gives you some cover with 'fishy' places like lily beds, reeds, overhanging willow trees and deeper water. Rivers offer a different challenge because they can be unpredictable and varied, depending on where you fish. Your local river may be fast flowing, ideal for fish such as grayling, chub, dace and barbel, or deep and slow, which is perfect for roach, rudd and bream. Canals are often narrow, shallow and slow moving and hold a wide variety of fish. If you live near a river or a canal, find out more about it at your local tackle shop or by talking to an angler on the bankside before you start fishing.

Many still waters are well kept and well stocked, with friendly staff on hand to give you advice and to help you. They offer a great place to start fishing.

Environment Savvy

1. Take all your rubbish home or put it in a rubbish bin. This includes old fishing line, weights and broken rigs, food wrappers and drinks cans.

2. Discarded fishing tackle is dangerous to wildlife – so bin it!

3. Make sure you fish in prepared swims to reduce damage to bankside vegetation and to avoid losing tackle.

4. Use barbless hooks (hooks without a second, backward pointing part) whenever possible.

5. Watch out for wildlife. Retrieve your line if birds are swimming nearby.

6. Do not leave your rod unattended.

7. Do not leave baited hooks on the river bank as they may be picked up by animals or birds.

Taking care of the environment

Fishing is a natural sport, and the best places to fish are often full of a wide variety of wild animals and plant life. A wildlife guidebook and a pair of binoculars will help you to identify some of the creatures with whom you share the waterside. Anglers need to learn to fish quietly and respect the natural environment. Fish will quickly become nervous and move away if you make a lot of noise, so, like a hunter, always move slowly and carefully, disturbing as little as possible.

The weather

As fishing is an all-year-round outdoor pursuit, weather plays a big part, so always be prepared. Try to find out about the expected weather before you go fishing and always wear the right clothing. Wellington boots or strong shoes with good grip are essential. Take a waterproof coat with you, just in case the weather turns. In winter, wear a layered clothing system to keep you warm and dry. In really hot spells, save your fishing for the early morning and evening when the fish will feed. Use an umbrella for shade and a good sun cream to avoid sunburn. Do not fish during thunderstorms because fishing rods make very good lightning conductors! Instead, wait for the storm to pass and then get ready for some excellent fishing.

Put all your rubbish in a bin before you leave the swim. If there is no bin nearby, be sure to take your litter home with you.

Fishing equipment

At first glance, the range of equipment, or tackle, that you can buy may seem overwhelming. But fishing is a simple sport – the basic tackle that you will need is fairly cheap and the skills that will help to get you started are quite easy to learn.

Rods – today's rods are made from a lightweight material such as carbon fibre, with handles made from cork or another waterproof material. Poles come in different lengths, and can be up to nearly 8 metres. The pole sections fit inside one another and are taken apart to allow the fish to be landed.

Reels – start by using a basic, fixed spool reel. The spool holds the line, while the bale arm traps the line for winding in and releasing for casting. The drag allows a strong fish to take line when it is hooked and stops the line breaking. Set the drag so that the line is not too easy to pull off the spool but so that it will not break when a strong fish tries to run.

Line – fishing line comes in a variety of strengths or 'breaking strains'. A good starting line for general fishing is about 1.3 kilograms. To load the reel, attach the line from the spool to the reel with a half blood knot (see page 11) and have someone hold the spool quite tightly while you reel it onto the spool carefully, making sure there is some tension so that it goes on neatly. Fill the reel to the lip of the spool.

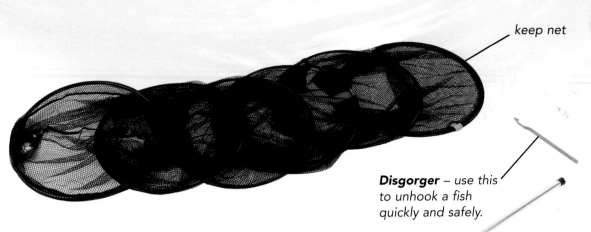

keep net

Disgorger – use this to unhook a fish quickly and safely.

Nets – a keep net allows you to retain your fish for the day so that you can see what you have caught. If you are fishing in a competition, it also allows you to have your catch weighed. A landing net is essential and will allow you to land a good fish safely and easily once it is played out.

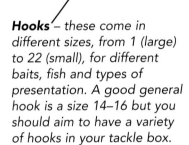

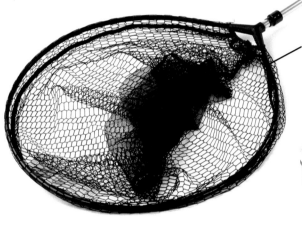

landing net

Hooks – these come in different sizes, from 1 (large) to 22 (small), for different baits, fish and types of presentation. A good general hook is a size 14–16 but you should aim to have a variety of hooks in your tackle box.

Bait box – this is used to store bait.

Floats – a few floats of different weights and sizes will get you started. A float allows you to present the bait to the fish at different levels in the water. Floats are also used to indicate a bite, which is why they are usually bright and highly visible. Floats are held down using weights called split shots, which are made of non-toxic metal. The amount of weight needed to cock the float will be printed on the side of the float. The largest (AAA) are called swan shot and the smallest (no10) are called dust shot.

Catapult – use this with care to get loose feed out to your fishing spot with accuracy and distance.

Ledger weights – ledger weights take the bait to the bottom of the water and hold it there. You will need ledger weights if you fish in deep water and/or on windy days. Weights include arlsey bombs, coffin leads and drilled bullets.

coffin leads

arlsey bombs

drilled bullets

Types of fish

There are many different types of fish that can be caught using simple tackle. In addition to those illustrated here, there are many more that are worth reading up about. These include the little gudgeon, the powerful barbel, the beautiful grayling and a real monster... the massive catfish.

Tench

Specimen: 1.3 kg

Record: 6.5 kg

Location: Still waters, canals and rivers

Tactics: Bottom feeders, ledgering or a float with the bait right on the bottom

Line: 2–2.5 kg

Hook size: 6–10

Bait: Worms, bread paste, sweetcorn, luncheon meat or maggots

Roach

Specimen: 1 kg

Record: 1.9 kg

Location: Rivers, canals, ponds and lakes

Tactics: Float fishing or ledgering

Line: 1–1.5 kg

Hook size: 14–20

Bait: Bread flake or paste, single maggot or cloudy mix groundbait

Bream

Specimen: 1.8 kg

Record: 8.3 kg

Location: Slow rivers, canals and lakes

Tactics: Bottom feeders or ledgering

Line: 1.3–1.9 kg

Hook size: 8–12

Bait: Worms, maggots, bread paste or flake

Carp

Specimen: 2 kg

Record: 30 kg

Location: Still waters, canals and rivers

Tactics: Floats, poles, ledgering, freelining or surface fishing

Line: 2 kg (4 kg and a powerful rod for bigger fish)

Hook size: 4–12

Bait: Worms, sweetened bread paste, sweetcorn, luncheon meat, bread crust, dog biscuits or boilies

Pike

Specimen: 5 kg

Record: 21 kg

Location: Rivers, weirs, reed beds, lakes, canals and reservoirs

Tactics: Ledgering, float fishing or spinning. Use a wire trace to stop the pike biting through the line.

Line: 5 kg

Hook size: Treble hook in 6–12

Bait: Small dead fish such as sprats, pilchards, mackerel or roach

Perch

Specimen: 1 kg

Record: 2.5 kg

Location: Lakes ponds, canals and slower, deeper, rivers

Tactics: Float fishing, ledgering or spinning

Line: 1.5 kg

Hook size: 8–14

Bait: Worms, maggots or spinners with a wire trace only

Unhooking Perch

Perch have sharp spines on their dorsal fin (the main fin on the spine). To unhook the fish, sweep the fin down from the head, pressing the spines down flat towards the tail. Hold the fish firmly on the side while taking out the hook.

Bait

Different types of fish prefer different baits. Depending on what you are hoping to catch, you will need to prepare a range of bait, from maggots and worms to corn and bread.

Maggots

Most fish will bite if you use maggots as bait. Maggots are the small, wriggly grubs of bluebottle flies. If you look closely enough, you will see that a maggot has a blunt end and a sharp end. To secure your bait, place the hook through the skin gently at the blunt end.

Bread

Bread is very good bait for roach, rudd, carp, tench and bream. It can be used in flakes, crusts or pastes to secure your catch. Try cutting up the crust in cubes as big as your thumb and using them on the surface of the water for carp. Bread flake is made by taking a pinch of bread from the middle of a white loaf and squeezing it onto the hook to leave it fluffy and attractive to the fish. Try making bread paste by taking a big slice of white bread without the crusts, wrapping it in a cloth and wetting it with water from your swim. Squeeze it until it forms a firm paste, then mould it onto the hook. You could add honey or other flavours to the bread to tempt fish.

Worms

Fish love worms! Lobworms are one of the biggest garden varieties and are great bait for carp, tench, bream, eels, perch and barbel. Red worms and brandlings are often found in good compost heaps and are smaller and attractive to many fish.

Sweetcorn

Buy large-grain sweetcorn and put one or more grains on the hook. Add some loose feed and the sweet smell will attract carp, tench, roach and bream.

Luncheon meat

Meat is a great bait for big fish such as carp, tench, barbel and bream. Cut the meat into cubes and thread the hook through it carefully. Fish the bait with a ledger rig (see page 23) and add a few pieces as loose feed to attract big fish.

Cheese

If you are after chub, try cheese. A small piece of hard cheese, such as Cheddar, moulded onto the hook will work wonders.

Fish

If you want to catch pike, a small fish, such as mackerel, is the bait to use. Pike are sometimes called freshwater sharks because of their size, strength and sharp teeth.

Boilies, dog biscuits, pepperoni

Flavoured baits, including pastes, pellets and boilies, are very popular and many varieties can be bought from a tackle shop.

Groundbait

Groundbait is essential because it attracts fish into your swim and keeps them there. Buy bags of ready-made groundbait at your tackle shop – the cheapest is breadcrumbs. Mix the groundbait with water to form a ball that can be loose to make a cloudy mix or heavy to make a sinking mix that will get to the bottom of a river with a current. You can add flavours such as vanilla or strawberry to make your own secret recipe.

Using the equipment

Once you have the basic equipment, you can get ready to fish! Set up your tackle away from the water's edge. Take your time and think about the weather conditions, the water and the type of fish you hope to catch. When ready, you can move slowly into position.

Setting up

1

Put the rod sections together and fix the reel to the rod handle or butt.

2

Make sure all the rod eyes are in a straight line.

3

Open the bale arm on the reel so that the line pulls off the reel.

4

Thread the line through ALL of the rod eyes.

5

Attach the end rig for ledgering or float fishing, depending on what fish you want to catch.

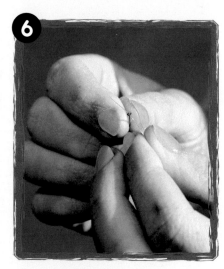

6

Tie on the hook.

Basic knots

Learn to tie these simple knots to ensure that your rig and hooks are secure.

Half blood knot

1

Thread the line through the eye and double up above it.

2

Twist the hook around eight times. Keep the twists tight and grab the loose end.

3

Push the hook through the lowest loop between the top of the eye and the first twist.

4

Push the loose end through the loop you have made. This is called the tuck.

5

Dampen the knot with a little spit and start to tighten it. Pull the knot down to the eye.

6

Hold the knot tight for three seconds, then trim it off.

Figure of eight knot

1

Make a simple loop at the end of the line.

2

Hook the loop over itself.

3

Put your index finger into the large loop and twist it around twice. Then make another half twist.

4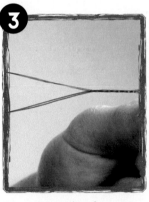

Tuck the small loop into the larger loop.

5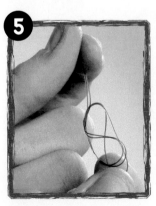

Tighten the knot and a figure of eight will form.

6

Add a little spit before you tighten up.

Basic techniques

Once you are familiar with your rod, tackle and types of bait, you should practise these techniques at home before you add a hook and head for the water.

Casting

Casting away from the bank will increase your chance of catching a fish. Always check that no one is standing behind you before you cast.

1. Wind the float to a point of about 5–7 cm beneath the rod tip and position your rod slightly in front of you to the right.

2. Open the bale arm so that the line is over your index finger.

3. Position the rod at 11 o'clock.

4. Decide where you want to cast, then push the rod tip forward firmly to 1 o'clock, at the same time as releasing the line off your finger. The weight of the tackle will carry the line forward towards the water.

5. When the bait hits the water, wind the float into position, sinking the line.

Hooking, playing and landing a fish

When you get a bite, you need to hook the fish. Bites can be quick or slow, gentle or powerful so always be prepared for action. If you hook a really big fish be extremely patient. Carefully use the rod and the reel drag to tire the fish until finally it is yours. Remember the golden rule: be patient!

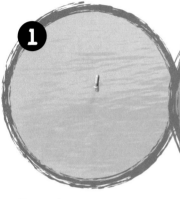

1

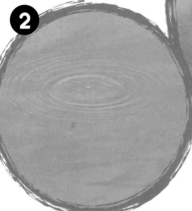

Be patient as you wait for a bite.

2

When the float dips below the water, you have a bite.

Lift the rod upwards smoothly and firmly – you should feel the fish pulling at the other end.

4

Wind in until the fish is over the landing net.

5

6

If it is a bigger fish, keep your rod high and wind in when the fish tires. Sink your landing net into the water.

Bring the fish into your net.

Practice Makes Perfect

Learn by practising at home. Get a friend to pretend to be the fish and practise reeling in and giving line as he or she pulls. Learn to get the tension on the reel drag right to let the line run out without snapping as the 'fish' runs away!

Unhooking and returning a fish

Having landed your fish, great care should be taken to unhook and return it to the water as quickly as possible. Before you put it back in the water, it is a good idea to take a photograph of your catch.

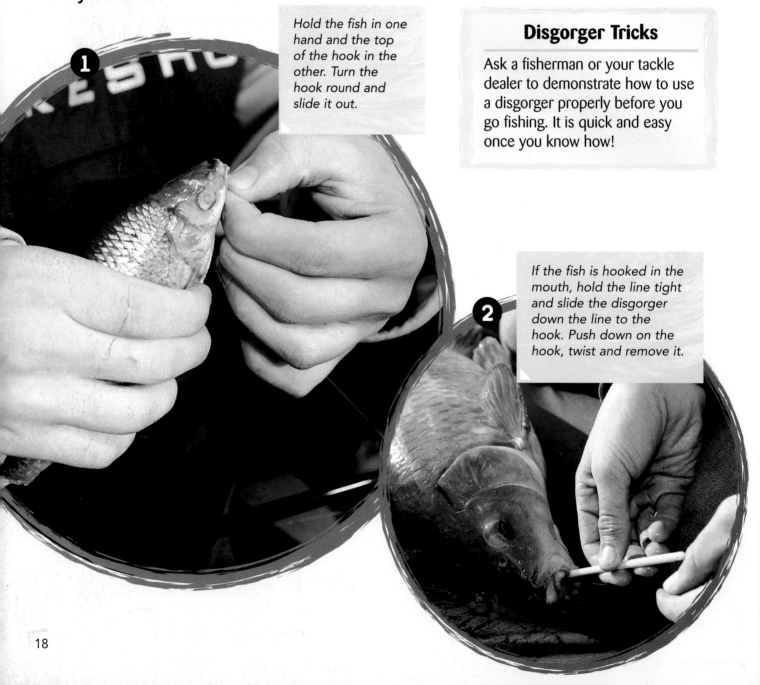

Hold the fish in one hand and the top of the hook in the other. Turn the hook round and slide it out.

Disgorger Tricks

Ask a fisherman or your tackle dealer to demonstrate how to use a disgorger properly before you go fishing. It is quick and easy once you know how!

If the fish is hooked in the mouth, hold the line tight and slide the disgorger down the line to the hook. Push down on the hook, twist and remove it.

3 Carefully put the fish into the keep net.

4 Larger fish can be unhooked on a damp fishing mat.

5 Weigh your catch using a weigh sling. Then, if you like, take a photograph of the fish.

6 Nurse the fish in the water for a moment before releasing it – do not release it until you feel its strength return.

19

Location, location, location

Where you fish will determine what technique you will use. Wherever you fish, make sure you are allowed to do so and obtain the necessary licences and permits.

Stillwater fishing

Ponds, lakes, pits and reservoirs are known as still waters because, unlike rivers, they do not have a current. This makes fishing easier and still water a good place to learn basic fishing skills. Find out all you can about the water you have chosen before you actually go. Take the time to talk to the local tackle shop or visit the water and talk to fishermen who are on the banks. Check out the cost of tickets, types of fish stocked, the best areas to fish from, and the most popular baits used.

At the waterside, pay attention to the features of the area. It is a good idea to make your own map of the water and keep a record of what you catch and where you catch it. Remember that fish like cover and stillness, so look for features such as reed beds, lily pads and overhanging trees. Fish close in to the bank using simple float fishing tackle and maggots, attracting the fish with groundbait. For deeper water and distance fishing, ledgering will be a better option. In high summer, where carp are present, surface fishing using bread or dog biscuits is one of the most exciting ways to catch fish.

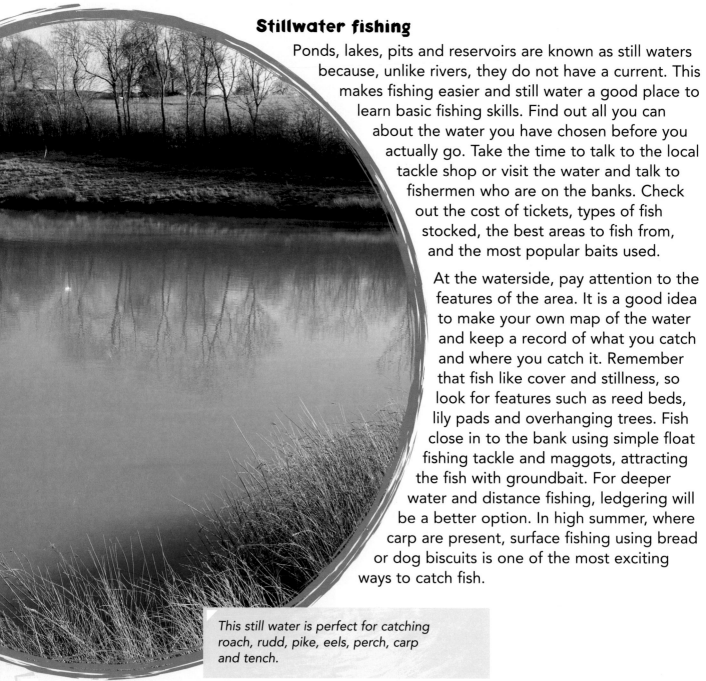

This still water is perfect for catching roach, rudd, pike, eels, perch, carp and tench.

Rivers and canals

Once you have mastered the basic skills in still waters, you can move on to rivers and canals.

Rivers can be shallow or deep, slow moving or fast and your tactics will depend on the type of river and the fish you want to catch. Start by fishing quite near to the bank so that you can easily control the float with your rod. Stronger currents may require a heavier float to get the bait down to the fish. Remember that the current will move the float downstream and this will require control on your part. Throw in groundbait and loose feed upstream of your swim and in line with the place that you want to fish, so that the offering arrives at the depth and place where you want to fish. In faster water let the bait roll downstream or wave in the current enticingly.

This fisherman has thrown some groundbait upstream of where he is fishing. The bait should attract fish, making a catch more likely.

Canals are usually slow moving and shallow. Fishing either up or downstream of your swim is a good idea to avoid scaring the fish. Canals can look featureless but you will attract fish into your swim with groundbait and loose feed.

This canal looks calm and featureless but there is a wealth of fish lurking below the water's surface.

Types of fishing

There are different types of fishing and, depending on the type of fish you are hoping to catch and the location of your swim, you may want to try a variety of methods.

Surface fishing

Surface fishing is exciting and a great way to catch carp in high summer. Throw in some loose feed and watch for tell-tale swirls. Cast out and wait – it will be only a matter of time before the carp suck in the bait and fight hard.

Float fishing

Float fishing uses brightly coloured and highly visible floats (see page 9). These allow you to fish your bait at different depths in the water. Floats also help you to detect bites easily. There are many floats to choose from but you can start with a couple of simple patterns and build up your collection. It is very important to find out the depth of the water in your swim. For this you can use a special weight called a plummet.

Use a plummet to find out the depth of water in your swim. The fish may be feeding near the bottom or high up in the water.

Floating on the Water

A float is set correctly if you can see just the tip of the float above the water's surface.

Ledgering

Ledgering takes the bait to the bottom of the water. It is used to catch bigger fish and is a great method to use in deep water, for distance fishing and for fishing a strong current, such as a river.

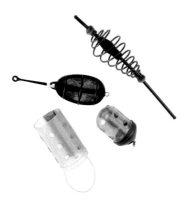

These are swimfeeders. They are used in ledgering to hold bait at the bottom of the water.

Freelining

This stillwater tactic uses no weight except the bait itself. It is successful, especially for carp and tench, because it presents the bait so naturally. Throw in some loose feed, such as sweetcorn, near reeds or other fishy spot close to the bank, put a few particles on the hook and lower the bait down. There is no need to cast. Sit well back, be patient and watch the line for sudden movement.

This is a simple ledger rig. You can vary the hook length to change presentation.

Fly fishing and sea fishing

Once you have tried coarse fishing and feel confident, then why not try fly fishing for trout, or sea fishing off the coast?

Fly fishing

There are many places to try fly fishing. Lakes are a good place to learn the basic techniques and are usually stocked with hard-fighting rainbow trout. Some lakes may be stocked with other varieties, too, such as browns, blues and tigers. Although there are some similarities between coarse and fly fishing, there are also some differences, and you will need to learn a new set of casting in skills.

Fly fishing is a wonderful branch of the sport. River fishing for trout can get you really close to the fish!

Flies

One of the most obvious differences between coarse and fly fishing is that instead of using floats, fly fishermen use flies, which are designed to catch trout. While some resemble natural flies, other fly patterns do not look anything like real flies! They are very gaudy and work by triggering the trout's attack mode. The trick is to learn about the insect life near the water you are fishing and try to trick the trout by imitating the insects.

This is a range of fly patterns for trout. Some flies try to imitate insects whilst others have gaudy colours to trigger the trout's attack mode.

Sea fishing

If you live near the sea or go there on holiday then why not try sea fishing? Fish can be caught from jetties, piers, harbour walls, beaches, rocks and boats. Your equipment will vary depending on the place you want to fish. For example, shorter rods are suitable for harbour walls and jetties while shore and rock fishing will require something longer. A 7-kilogram line loaded onto a fixed-spool reel, along with a small assortment of tackle and bait, will be enough to get you started.

weights – *these are bigger than freshwater weights so that they can cope with the surges in tides.*

bucket – *you need this to keep your catch.*

beachcaster and deep-sea rod *– sea rods vary in length and power.*

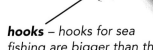

floats *– these are useful for harbour and rock fishing.*

hooks *– hooks for sea fishing are bigger than those used for coarse fishing.*

baits *– fish-like baits are best for sea fishing.*

25

Clubs and competitions

There are fishing clubs all over the world and many will cover all aspects of fishing. Some local clubs may support a match-fishing team while others specialise in catching particular fish, such as the Pike Angler's Club of Great Britain and The National Anguila Club which specialises in catching eels. The best way to find a club is to speak to your local tackle shop, by visiting the library or going online.

There are many advantages to joining a club. Not only do clubs offer access to 'members only' private lakes and stretches of river, but many will also run competitions that you can enter. Much can be learnt from more experienced club members and some clubs will offer tuition for more junior or inexperienced members.

By joining a club, expert help will be on hand. Here, a bailiff is offering advice to a girl on where to fish.

Competitions

Competition or match fishing is a popular and very successful branch of the sport. There are hundreds of individual and team competitions held every week. Match fishing offers a unique challenge to anglers. At a match, anglers draw a 'peg' or swim before the start of the competition and then fish against each other, against other teams and against the clock to catch the heaviest weight of fish over the day. Match fishing provides every competitor with the chance to be their best at the sport and to learn from those around them. Fishing as part of a team can be a great experience and may lead to strong and lasting friendships – not to mention winning a trophy!

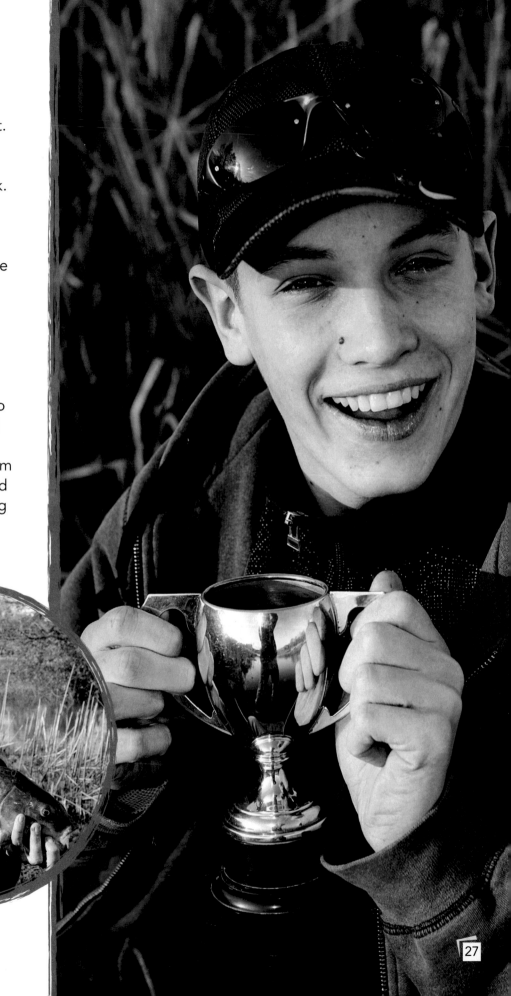

This carp put up a real fight and was big enough to win a cup for this young angler in a local fishing match.

Fish from around the world

Around the world, certain waters are known for their fishing. There is something for everyone, whichever type of fishing you enjoy most.

Coarse fishing

All over the United Kingdom, carp fishing is really popular, but if you want to fish for really big carp, the best place to do this is Bangkok in Thailand. There, the biggest carp ever caught on a rod and line weighed over 110 kilograms. Spain's River Ebro is a good place to fish giant catfish. Catfish are predators, and are generally caught using fish baits at night. In 2005, a catfish the size of a grizzly bear was caught in Thailand. The fish was 2.7 metres long and weighed 293 kilograms. It took a team of anglers over an hour to land the fish.

While fishermen dream of catching a world record breaker, beating your own record is exciting. This angler was very pleased with his own record-breaking carp that weighed in at just under 10 kilograms.

Although this feisty 5-kilogram pike put up a good fight, it was worth it in the end!

Fly fishing

If you like fly fishing then you could try going for the giant steelhead of Canada and the USA. The US record fish was caught in Alaska and weighed in at just over 19 kilograms. Giant tarpon are found off the coast of Florida, USA. These enormous fish weigh up to 100 kilograms and are caught from boats in shallow waters called 'flats' using fly fishing tackle. Salmon from the Kola Peninsula in Northern Russia are amongst the best in the world, with fish taken to over 18 kilograms that will test even the strongest tackle.

Sea fishing

Some of the biggest fish in the world can be caught near the Great Barrier Reef in Australia. There, giant black marlins are common. The biggest caught to date off the reef weighed an incredible, 550 kilograms.

This fisherman is nursing the trout he has caught before putting it back.

This big black marlin was caught off the Queensland coast in Australia.

Glossary

Bait The things that fish like to eat, such as maggots, corn or cheese. By using diffrent bait, you will attract different types of fish.

Bale arm An arm that clicks over on the spool of your reel and collects the line onto the spool when you turn the handle.

Bite When a fish takes your bait.

Boilies A specialist, high-protein bait for carp fishing. Boilies are usually coloured and strongly flavoured.

Breaking strain The limit of strain that a fishing line can take before it snaps. Fishing line comes in a wide variety of strengths and you can ask your tackle shop for advice on the best line to use for the fish you want to catch.

Carbon fibre A special material that is very light but incredibly strong. Modern fishing rods are made from carbon fibre.

Coarse fishing Fishing for freshwater fish, such as carp.

Downstream The direction in which water naturally flows.

Drag This is the setting on the reel that increases or decreases the level of resistance that the fish feels when taking line. If a strong fish pulls or runs suddenly, drag allows the line to be released without snapping.

Featureless Without any features. Canal waters often look featureless because they are calm and flat.

Flies The lures that fly fishermen use to catch trout and salmon. The flies are made to look like natural flies or they are very bright to provoke the trout's attack mode.

Floats The devices used to present the bait at different levels. They are also used to indicate a bite. Floats are coloured on one half so that you can see them clearly but they are dull on the other side so that they do not discourage fish.

Float fishing A fishing tactic that uses floats to show whether or not there is a bite.

Fly fishing Fishing for salmon and trout. Fly fishermen use artificial flies instead of bait.

Freelining A fishing tactic that uses no weight except the bait itself.

Fresh water Rivers, canals, ponds and lakes are all bodies of fresh water.

Industrial Revolution The time in history in the late eighteenth and early nineteenth centuries when major changes in manufacturing, farming and transportation took place. After the Revolution many things were made in factories.

Keep net The net used to keep a fish that you have caught.

Landing a fish When you have caught a fish and have got it safely on the bank, you have landed it.

Landing net The net used to bring the fish to land.

Ledgering A fishing tactic where anglers fish on the bottom of the water.

Lightning conductor Something that allows lightning to travel through it, for example a fishing rod.

Match fishing Competition fishing where fishermen draw pegs to find out where they need to fish. Prizes are awarded for the biggest fish.

Playing out Once the fish has bitten, it will fight so that it is not caught. Loosening and tightening the line to bring it in is called playing it out.

Rig The line, float and hook used in fishing.

Spinning A tactic used to catch pike that uses artificial lures, called spinners or plugs, which act like wounded or injured fish in the water, provoking a bite.

Spool This is where the line sits on your reel. Most reels come with more that one spool and they can easily be changed. It is useful to have more than one spool for your reel with different weights of line for different fish and different conditions.

Surface fishing A fishing tactic where anglers use bait that floats, such as bread crust or dog biscuits, to catch surface-feeding fish. It is an especially good tactic for catching carp.

Swimfeeder A special device that is used to hold groundbait when you fish on the bottom to get feed close to your hook bait.

Swims Parts along a river or other body of water where you can fish.

Trace line Made of wire or coated plastic, a trace should be used when pike fishing as the fish will not be able to bite through it.

Upstream The opposite direction to the natural flow of water.

Weir A dam built across a river to raise the level of water upstream or regulate its flow.

Further information

Books to read

Coarse Fishing Basics: A Beginner's Guide Steve Partner, Hamlyn (2006)

How to Go Fishing and Catch Fish Gareth Purnell, Franklin Watts (2007)

Usborne First Skills: Starting Fishing L Sims and H Edon, Usborne (2004)

Useful contacts

International Carp Fishing Association
www.icfa.info

The Australian Trout and Freshwater Angling Association
www.watfaa.iinet.net.au

The American Sportfishing Association
www.asafishing.org

National Junior Angling Association in the UK
www.njaa.org.uk

British Disabled Angling is a registered charity that helps develop fishing opportunities for people with disabilities.
www.bdaa.co.uk

Websites

This website has all the information you will need to go fishing, from equipment and licences to competitions and online shopping. Log on at:
http://www.fishing.co.uk

For lots of information on coarse fishing, log on to this website:
www.coarsefish.net

Anglers Mail *weekly fishing magazine is filled with all the latest news from the world of fishing. If your local newsagents do not stock it, you can read an electonic edition at:*
www.anglersmail.co.uk

This website has lots of information on trout and salmon fishing, including an online book store and tackle shop. Log on at:
www.trout-salmon-fishing.com

index

Ancient Egypt 5
Australia 29

bait 7, 9, 10, 11, 12–13, 16, 20, 21, 22, 23, 25, 30
bait boxes 9
bale arms 8, 14, 16, 30
barbel 6, 10, 12, 13
binoculars 7
bites 9, 17, 22, 30
black marlins 29
bream 6, 10, 12, 13

Canada 29
canals 6, 10, 11, 21
carp 11, 12, 13, 20, 22, 23, 27, 28
casting in 8, 16, 22, 24
catapult 9
catfish 10, 28
chub 6, 13
clothes 7
clubs 6, 26
competitions 9, 26, 27

dace 6
disgorger 9, 18

eels 12, 20, 26
equipment 4, 5, 8–9, 14–15
    sea fishing equipment 25
    see also individual pieces

flies 25, 30
float fishing 10, 11, 20, 22, 30
floats 9, 10, 11, 16, 17, 21, 25, 30
fly fishing 4, 24–25, 29, 30

freelining 11, 23, 30
fresh water fishing 4

game fishing 4
grayling 6, 10
gudgeon 10

hooking a fish 17
hooks 4, 7, 9, 10, 11, 12, 13, 14, 15, 16, 17, 18, 25

knots 8, 15

lakes 6, 10, 20, 24, 26
landing fish 8, 9, 17, 18, 28, 30
ledgering 10, 11, 14, 20, 23, 30
licences 6, 20
lines 5, 7, 8, 10, 11, 14, 15, 16, 17, 18, 25, 26, 30

match fishing 5, 26, 27, 30

nets 9, 17, 19, 30
nursing fish 19, 29

perch 11, 12, 20
photographs 18, 19
pike 11, 13, 20, 28
ponds 6, 10, 20

reed beds 11, 20
reel drag 17
reels 8, 14, 17, 25, 30
reservoirs 11, 20
returning fish 18, 19, 29
rigs 7, 14, 23, 24

rivers 6, 10, 11, 20, 21, 23, 24, 26, 28
roach 6, 10, 11, 12, 20
rods 4, 7, 8, 14, 16, 17, 21, 25, 28
rudd 6, 12, 20
Russia 29

salmon 4, 29
sea fishing 4, 24, 25, 29
setting up a rig 14
Spain 28
spinning 11, 30
split shot 9
steelhead 29
surface fishing 11, 20, 22
swimfeeders 23, 30
swims 6, 7, 12, 13, 21, 22, 27, 30

tackle 5, 7, 8, 9, 10, 14, 16, 20, 25, 29
tackle shops 6, 13, 20, 26, 30
tarpon 29
techniques 4, 10, 11, 16–17, 20, 24
tench 10, 12, 13, 20, 23
Thailand 28
trout 4, 24, 25
types of fish 10–11
    see also individual types

unhooking fish 11, 18–19, 30
United Kingdom 4, 28
USA 29

weather 5, 7
weighing fish 19
weights 7, 9, 10, 22, 23, 30
weirs 11, 30